GEO
NA
USA PARKS
THEODORE
Theodore Roose

Theodore Roosevelt National Park

John Hamilton

National Parks

Published by ABDO Publishing Company, 8000 West 78th Street, Suite 310, Edina, MN 55439.

Copyright ©2009 by Abdo Consulting Group, Inc. International copyrights reserved in all countries.

No part of this book may be reproduced in any form without written permission from the publisher.

ABDO & Daughters™ is a trademark and logo of ABDO Publishing Company.

Printed in the United States.

Editor: Sue Hamilton

Graphic Design: John Hamilton

All photos and illustrations by the author, except p. 5, Theodore Roosevelt portrait, Library of Congress; p. 6, Elkhorn Ranch Unit, Department of the Interior; p. 15, map, National Park Service; p. 16 Theodore Roosevelt in buckskin, National Park Service; p. 18 Theodore Roosevelt with horse, National Park Service; p. 26, North Unit, Comstock; p. 29 elk, iStockphoto.

Library of Congress Cataloging-in-Publication Data

Hamilton, John, 1959-
  Theodore Roosevelt National Park / John Hamilton.
      p. cm. -- (National parks)
  Includes index.
  ISBN 978-1-60453-095-7
  1. Theodore Roosevelt National Park (N.D.)--Juvenile literature. I. Title.

F642.T5H36 2009
978.4'94--dc22

                              2008011893

Contents

A view of the badlands from **Painted Canyon Overlook.**

Rugged Beauty

Entering North Dakota's Theodore Roosevelt National Park is like stepping into a time machine. The badlands are scraped away from the surrounding plains, unveiling millions of years of history. Layers of sedimentary rock, in a rainbow of yellows, browns, and reds, reveal the area's prehistoric origins. Weird-looking mesas, buttes, and valleys, sculpted by eons of water and wind, seem transported from the moon. But unlike that lifeless place, there are many creatures and plants that live in the park. Bison, elk, prairie dogs, prickly pear cactus, and even wild horses thrive here.

Theodore Roosevelt National Park is also a place where history has been preserved and honored. The park's namesake was the 26th president of the United States, a leader who did much to preserve this country's natural beauty for future generations. During his time in office, Theodore Roosevelt founded the U.S. Forest Service. He also established 5 national parks and 18 national monuments. As a young

man, Roosevelt spent time in the badlands of today's western North Dakota, living the rugged life of a rancher, hunter, and law enforcer. He credited his time in Dakota Territory with influencing the kind of man he would later become. "I never would have been President," he once said, "if it had not been for my experiences in North Dakota."

Left: President Theodore Roosevelt.

Established in 1978, today's national park is made up of three parts totaling 70,447 acres (28,509 ha). The South Unit is the most visited because it lies next to Interstate 94, a major road that runs east and west through North Dakota. The main visitor center is on the edge of Medora, a pleasant little town that holds tight to its Wild West roots.

The slightly smaller North Unit is about 70 miles (113 km) north of Medora on Highway 85. It's less visited, but considered by many to be the most beautiful. It's certainly less crowded. On some off-season days, visitors can feel like they have the park to themselves.

The park's third unit is the most isolated of all. Situated halfway between the South and North Units, the Elkhorn Ranch Unit preserves the site of Theodore Roosevelt's "home ranch," which he called the Elkhorn. Nothing remains of the ranch house that used to stand there, but foundation blocks mark its outline. Travel on a bumpy dirt road, a river crossing, and a three-mile (4.8-km) roundtrip hike are required to reach the unit, but it's well worth the effort to retrace the footsteps of Roosevelt himself. The area is mostly unchanged from the time he worked on his ranch, giving visitors a taste of what the great president must have experienced in this starkly beautiful landscape.

Left: A panoramic view of the Elkhorn Ranch Unit, where Theodore Roosevelt worked on one of his two ranches in the North Dakota badlands.

A bison grazes in front of a butte in the **South Unit.**

A Bizarre Landscape

Theodore Roosevelt called the North Dakota badlands "fantastically beautiful." At first glance, some visitors might disagree, thinking that the earth here has been torn apart by a natural disaster, such as an earthquake. But the landscape was formed by something even more powerful: the slow and unrelenting forces of erosion.

The history of Theodore Roosevelt National Park goes back more than 60 million years. To the west, the Rocky Mountains were recently arisen. Sediments from their eroded foothills began settling downstream on a huge, level plain. Over millions of years, layer upon layer of silt, sand, and clay covered the entire western half of North Dakota, as well as neighboring states and parts of Canada. These layers are clearly visible today in the park's buttes and eroded hills.

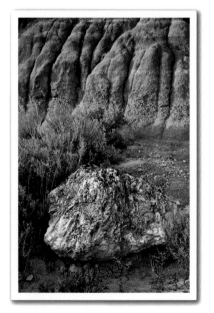

The climate was much different in prehistoric times from the dry, arid conditions the area experiences today. We know there was once a warm, subtropical climate here because of fossils that have been unearthed, including giant trees, turtles, and crocodiles. Dense forests of sequoia and cypress trees lived and died in this ancient wetland region. In fact, one of the largest deposits of petrified wood in the United States is found in the park.

Left: A petrified tree stump, probably an ancient type of sequoia, found along the road in the South Unit.

Layers of **sedimentary rock** are clearly visible in the badlands.

For many thousands of years, dying plants fell to the bottom of the shallow water. The dead matter accumulated, and was compacted further by more and more layers of sediments and volcanic ash. The plants were finally pressed so tightly and for so long that they transformed into a kind of coal called lignite. These black coal layers are easily visible today. Sometimes, lightning ignites the exposed coal. When a coal bed burns, it bakes the layer of sediment above it, leaving behind a rich red rock called porcelanite (incorrectly called scoria by some people).

Eventually, erosion ate away at the rocks. The Little Missouri River once flowed north all the way to Hudson Bay, in northern Canada. About 600,000 years ago, ice-age glaciers blocked the river, forcing it to turn eastward and empty into the Mississippi River. By the time the glaciers retreated, the river's course had been set. Its flow was steeper now, and the rushing water easily cut deeply into the soft sedimentary layers, creating the strange-looking badland formations.

This erosion process is ongoing. Each day, the Little Missouri River cuts slightly deeper into the landscape. Every time it rains, gullies widen. Every time water freezes and thaws, it breaks down the rocks and soil. Every time the wind blows, dust and sand sculpt the rocks into weird-looking spires. When you visit Theodore Roosevelt National Park, look closely—it will never be quite the same way again, thanks to the relentless forces of erosion.

Left: The Little Missouri River continually cuts through the park's soft, sedimentary layers of rock.

Burning coal caused the red rock visible from **Scoria Point Overlook**

—Theodore Roosevelt *(Above: A herd of bison wander over a ridge in the South Unit.)*   13

History in the Park

At 2:00 A.M. on September 8, 1883, Theodore Roosevelt stepped off a Northern Pacific steam train in the village of Little Missouri, on the western edge of Dakota Territory. He stood alone on the dark train platform, then made his way to a nearby hotel, sleeping on a dirty cot in a loft with cowboys and drifters. The next morning he arose, ready for adventure.

Roosevelt was a 24-year-old, Harvard-educated New Yorker from a wealthy family. He was skinny, with narrow shoulders and thick eyeglasses. He didn't seem cut out for life on the frontier. Local people made fun of his designer buckskin shirt and his ritzy department-store knife. But what he lacked in physical stature, the self-assured young man made up for with determination. Soon, "four-eyes" Roosevelt earned the respect of the local people. He was quiet and easy to get along with, but he was also tough, always willing to get his hands dirty.

Left: The visitor center in Medora, North Dakota, contains a fine collection of Theodore Roosevelt's hunting rifles and other items from his days in the badlands.

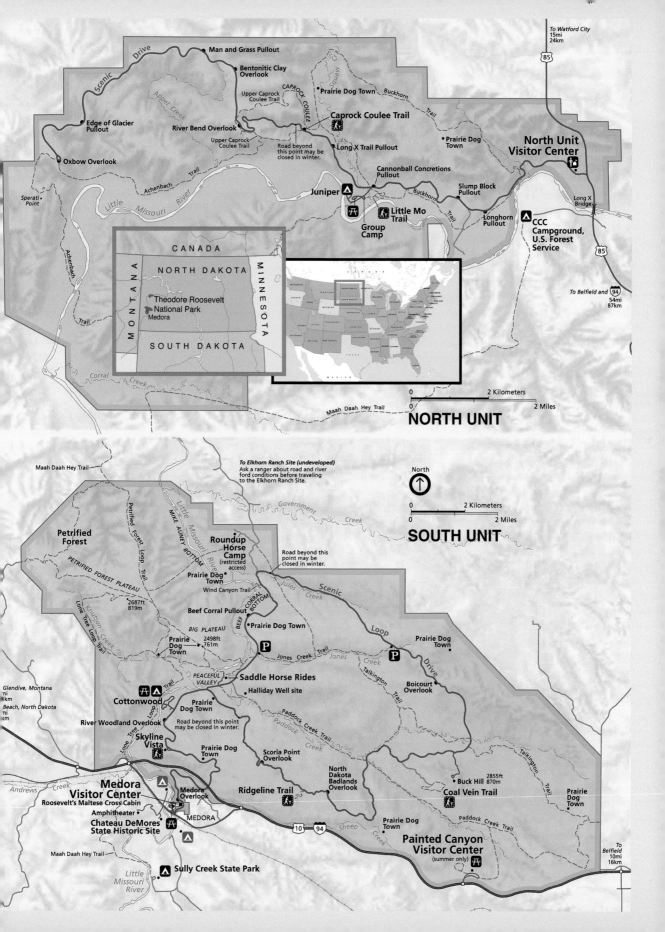

NORTH UNIT

To Watford City
15mi
24km

85

Man and Grass Pullout

Bentonitic Clay
Overlook

Upper Caprock
Coulee Trail

CAPROCK COULEE

Prairie Dog Town

Buckhorn

Caprock Coulee Trail

Appel Creek

Scenic Drive

Edge of Glacier
Pullout

River Bend Overlook

Upper Caprock
Coulee Trail

Road beyond
this point may be
closed in winter.

Long X Trail Pullout

Prairie Dog
Town

North Unit
Visitor Center

Oxbow Overlook

Achenbach Trail

Cannonball Concretions
Pullout

Juniper

Buckhorn

Slump Block
Pullout

Longhorn
Pullout

Long X
Bridge

Little Missouri River

Little Mo
Trail

Group
Camp

CCC
Campground,
U.S. Forest
Service

85

To Belfield and
54mi
87km

94

Sperati
Point

Achenbach
Trail

CANADA

NORTH DAKOTA

MONTANA   MINNESOTA

Theodore Roosevelt
National Park
Medora

SOUTH DAKOTA

Corral
Creek

Maah Daah Hey Trail

0   2 Kilometers
0   2 Miles

SOUTH UNIT

Maah Daah Hey Trail

To Elkhorn Ranch Site (undeveloped)
Ask a ranger about road and river
ford conditions before traveling
to the Elkhorn Ranch Site.

Government   Creek

North
↑
0   2 Kilometers
0   2 Miles

Petrified
Forest

Petrified Forest Loop Trail

MIKE AUNEY BOTTOM

Little Missouri River

Roundup
Horse
Camp
(restricted
access)

Prairie Dog
Town

Road beyond this
point may be
closed in winter.

PETRIFIED FOREST PLATEAU

2687ft
819m

Wind Canyon Trail

Beef Corral Pullout

BEEF CORRAL BOTTOM

Jules   Creek

Scenic

Knutson Creek

BIG PLATEAU

2498ft
761m

Prairie Dog Town

Loop

Prairie Dog Town

Lone Tree Loop Trail

Prairie
Dog
Town

P

Jones Creek Trail

Jones   Creek

P

Drive

Prairie Dog
Town

Glendive, Montana
ni
km

Beach, North Dakota
ni
km

PEACEFUL
VALLEY

Saddle Horse Rides

Halliday Well site

Talkington   Trail

Boicourt
Overlook

Cottonwood

Prairie
Dog Town

River Woodland Overlook

Road beyond
this point
may be
closed in winter.

Paddock   Creek   Trail

Paddock   Creek

Andrews   Creek

Skyline
Vista

Prairie Dog
Town

Scoria Point
Overlook

North
Dakota
Badlands
Overlook

Buck Hill

2855ft
870m

Prairie
Dog
Town

Lone Tree Loop Trail

Medora
Visitor Center
Roosevelt's Maltese Cross Cabin
Amphitheater
Chateau DeMores
State Historic Site

Medora
Overlook

MEDORA

Ridgeline Trail

Coal Vein Trail

Talkington Trail

10   94

Sheep   Creek

Prairie Dog
Town

Painted Canyon
Visitor Center
(summer only)

To
Belfield
10mi
16km

Maah Daah Hey Trail

Little
Missouri
River

Sully Creek State Park

Roosevelt came west to hunt bison. He wanted to experience the wild frontier before civilization swallowed it up. But by the time he got to Dakota Territory, most of the great herds had been wiped out by over-hunting and disease. He finally killed a bison after two weeks of hunting. During that time, he learned about cattle ranching, which was a growing industry in the area. He invested in the Maltese Cross Ranch, which was located about seven miles (11 km) south of the town of Medora. He had a cabin constructed in the woodsy bottomlands of the ranch. The three-room building was made of ponderosa pine logs, with wooden floors and a steeply pitched roof. In the attic was a loft where ranch hands could sleep.

During that first year of 1883, Roosevelt only stayed a few weeks before returning to New York. But he kept coming back for several years afterward, spending more and more time in the rugged badlands he grew to love. The life of a rancher suited Roosevelt. "I do not believe," he wrote, "there ever was any life more attractive to a vigorous young fellow than life on a cattle ranch in those days. It was a fine, healthy life, too; it taught a man self-reliance, hardihood, and the value of instant decision… I enjoyed the life to the full."

In the winter of 1884, Roosevelt's mother and his first wife, Alice, died on the same day. That June, the grief-stricken Roosevelt returned to Dakota Territory to heal his mental wounds. He started the Elkhorn Ranch about 35 miles (56 km) north of

Medora. He found the isolation he was looking for there. He raised cattle, and frequently hunted game in the rugged badlands. Although he kept partial ownership of the Maltese Cross Ranch, Roosevelt called the Elkhorn his "home ranch." He went back to New York rejuvenated, but returned several times over the next few years to his beloved badlands.

Left: Theodore Roosevelt poses in his buckskin outfit, along with his hunting rifle and knife.

Theodore Roosevelt's Maltese Cross cabin (above) has been relocated just behind the park visitor center in Medora. Some of Roosevelt's personal belongings are in the cabin (below).

Roosevelt with one of his horses.

During the harsh winter of 1886-87, Roosevelt lost more than half of his cattle. By this time, he had become very active in politics. By 1892, Roosevelt had sold most of his cattle business in Dakota Territory.

Life in the desolate, starkly beautiful badlands transformed Roosevelt. When he first arrived in 1883, he was intent on hunting bison and other big game. But he saw what had happened because of over-hunting. He also saw how civilization's unlimited growth spoiled the natural world. He was determined to preserve the special places that remained, "… keeping for our children's children… the burly majesty of the mightier forms of wildlife."

In 1901, Roosevelt became the 26th president of the United States. He laid the foundation for today's system of setting aside federal lands for future generations. He established the U.S. Forest Service in 1905. He used the 1906 Antiquities Act to create 18 national monuments. He signed into law five national parks. He also preserved millions of acres of land in more than 150 national forests and wildlife refuges. These and other accomplishments are why people call Roosevelt the "conservation president."

After Theodore Roosevelt's death in 1919, many people wanted to name a national park after him. The North Dakota badlands were a natural choice, but there were no established parklands at that time. Later, during the Great Depression of the 1930s, the federal government gave many people jobs to get them through the rough economic times. Roosevelt's fifth cousin, President Franklin D. Roosevelt, put people to work building roads, campgrounds, and picnic shelters in several wilderness areas, including the North Dakota badlands.

After World War II, Congress established Theodore Roosevelt National Memorial Park in 1947. On November 10, 1978, President Jimmy Carter signed a law making the area a national park. By setting aside these 70,447 acres (28,509 ha) of wilderness, the country officially recognized its importance as a national treasure, and honored the legacy of our conservation president, Theodore Roosevelt.

Wild horses roam free in Theodore Roosevelt National Park.

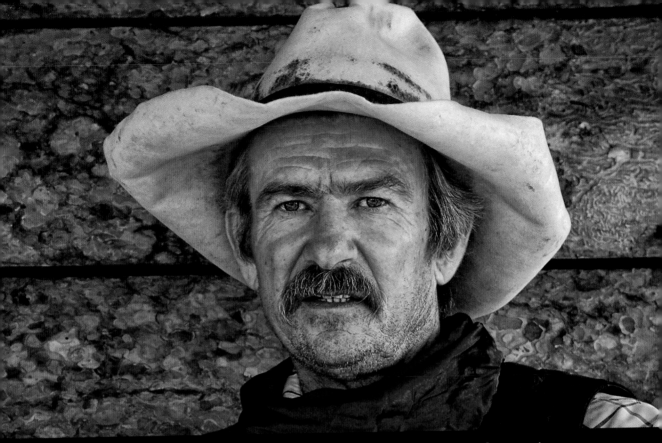

The spirit of Theodore Roosevelt is alive and well in the park. Real-life cowboys continue to work on area horse ranches (above). Caprock formations in the South Unit (below).

Light from a full winter moon illuminates the badlands in Painted Canyon (above).
A herd of bison (below) runs through the bottomlands near the Little Missouri River.

Plants and Wildlife

At first glance, you might think that nothing could live or grow in the forbidding landscape of the North Dakota badlands. But wander slowly

Cactus

through the park, or simply sit still for a while. You'll see that Theodore Roosevelt National Park is positively teeming with life.

There are more than 100 common plants that grow in the park, although in total it contains as many as 500 different plant species. Many of these are types of grasses, which thrive in the arid environment. The area only receives an average of about 15 inches (38 cm) of precipitation each year. Near river bottoms and shady hillsides, several types of trees grow, including cottonwoods, ash, willows, and dark green junipers. On hillsides facing the sun, sagebrush and hardier types of grasses are found. During springtime, after winter snows melt, yellow and red wildflowers bloom, adding even more color to the badlands.

Left: A bumblebee settles on a flowering plant in the park's South Unit.

There are more than 200 species of birds in the park. Many of them are songbirds. Theodore Roosevelt's favorite was the meadowlark, "one of our sweetest, loudest songsters," he once wrote.

Rabbit

Black-tailed prairie dogs are scattered throughout the park. Several prairie dog "towns" are easily seen from park roads. Feeding on these small rodents are prairie rattlesnakes, which are common in the park but rarely cause trouble for humans.

There are many types of larger animals that make the area their home. The park is most famous for its herds of bison, also known as buffalo. After being hunted to extinction in the park in late 19th century, these large herbivores were re-introduced in 1956. Today, more than 500 bison roam the North and South Units of the park.

Other animals in Theodore Roosevelt National Park include coyotes, bighorn sheep, elk, wild turkey, rabbits, pronghorn, deer, and wild (feral) horses.

Above: Adult male bison, such as this bull wandering along the shores of the Little Missouri River, can weigh as much as 2,000 pounds (907 kg).

Touring the Park

Theodore Roosevelt is one of the least-visited national parks in America, which is a very pleasant experience for those who take the time and effort to travel there. By far the most popular part of the park is the South Unit, located just off Interstate 94 in western North Dakota, adjacent to the town of Medora. When traveling west from Bismarck, North Dakota, the first view of the park is at the Painted Canyon Overlook. From the lip of the canyon, the panoramic views of the badlands give visitors a taste of what's to come.

A trip through the South Unit starts at the Medora Visitor Center. In addition to natural history displays and personal items owned by Theodore Roosevelt, visitors can take a tour of the Maltese Cross cabin. The wooden ranch house was Roosevelt's first home in the badlands, now located just behind the visitor center.

A 36-mile (58-km) road loops through the South Unit, perfect for touring the area's major sights. Interpretive signs and short walks are scattered along the way. At Skyline Vista, you can look down at the Little Missouri River and the colorful surrounding bluffs and buttes. After passing a prairie dog town, you come to River Woodland Overlook for a closer view of the broken badlands. Tall cottonwood trees grow near the river, providing shade for campgrounds. At Scoria Point, you are surrounded by the rich colors of badland formations. Ridgeline Trail, North Dakota Badlands Overlook, and Buck Hill provide opportunity for short hikes, as well as fabulous views of the park's vast beauty.

For those wishing to get off the road, there are miles of hiking trails crisscrossing the park. Bring plenty of water on hot summer days, and watch out for quickly developing thunderstorms. Horse rides are also available at Peaceful Valley Ranch, located in the middle of the South Unit.

Horse riders tour the park's South Unit on a warm, summer day.

Some people think that the North Unit is the more beautiful of the two main sections of the park. It is certainly the least crowded. During the off-season, you can spend all day sightseeing and barely bump into anybody else.

The North Unit is located about 70 miles (113 km) north of Medora, just south of Watford City on Highway 85. It's an out-of-the-way place, but well worth the time to visit. It is most easily explored by taking a 14-mile (23-km) scenic drive that starts at the visitor center. There are many places to get out of your car and hike on self-guided nature trails. The Caprock Coulee Trail is a 4-mile (6-km) trek through badland gulches, grassland plains, and hilltops with panoramic views. The end of the road climbs a ridge to Oxbow Overlook, with views of the Little Missouri River making a large bend as it winds its way through the badlands.

Many people don't realize that Theodore Roosevelt is an all-year park. Winter can be bone-chillingly cold, but the rewards are great. Not only do visitors have much of the park to themselves, they're treated to a kind of stark, isolated beauty that is seldom found anywhere else today.

Above: The Little Missouri River meanders through the North Unit.

Scattered throughout the park are **prairie dog towns.**

Future Challenges

Theodore Roosevelt National Park usually has very good air quality. Stargazers (not the Hollywood kind) are rewarded with clear views of the Milky Way and the northern lights. The U.S. Congress has designated that Theodore Roosevelt is a Class I air-quality area. That means it is supposed to be protected from any additional future air pollutants. In recent years, park officials have been concerned because of the construction of nearby coal-burning power plants. A coal gasification plant has been proposed only 15 miles (24 km) from the South Unit's boundary. Recent weakening of federal air-quality regulations have many people worried that the park's skies will someday become hazy. This is sometimes a problem in several parks, such as Grand Canyon and Death Valley National Parks.

Another problem facing park officials is managing the population of certain animals, such as prairie dogs, wild horses, elk, and bison. Theodore Roosevelt provides a sheltered habitat for these animals, but park resources can only support a certain number. For example, an adult bison bull can weigh up to 2,000 pounds (907 kg). These large herbivores eat a lot of grass. When their numbers get too many, some are rounded up and sold to outside organizations.

Left: A herd of bison creates a small traffic jam at the Cottonwood Campground.

Horses and elk, too, make their mark on the landscape. Elk populations have been especially troublesome in recent years. Elk have no natural predators in the park, and their numbers have been booming. Colorado's Rocky Mountain National Park has a similar elk problem. To control the herds, they selectively hunt some animals, and perform birth control procedures on some females. Officials in Theodore Roosevelt are considering similar methods to keep the park's elk population under control.

Elk

Officials are also struggling to control the number of exotic plants that have recently invaded the park. These are plants that are not native to the area ecosystem, such as leafy spurge, tamarisk, and Canada thistle. These and other non-native plants are very aggressive, spreading quickly and crowding out existing plants. To manage the invaders, park workers use cutting and chemical control. Sometimes, specially selected insects, whose diet includes the exotic plants, are released into the park. Biologists hope that the bugs feast only on the non-native plants. This method of control can be a nontoxic alternative to using chemicals, which might accidentally harm other plants and animals.

Left: Canada thistle is an example of what biologists call exotic plants, which aggressively compete with native plants for precious water and soil nutrients.

Glossary

Badlands

Badlands are geographic areas that have been heavily eroded, with little vegetation. Loose, sedimentary soil has been carved by erosion into fantastic shapes, with many mesas, steep slopes, and deep gullies. Spanish and French colonists in the New World called these regions "bad lands," or "bad land to cross." In North America, the most extensive badlands are located in western North and South Dakota, northwestern Nebraska, and parts of Saskatchewan and Alberta, Canada.

Ecosystem

A biological community of animals, plants, and bacteria, all of whom live together in the same physical or chemical environment.

Federal Lands

Much of America's land, especially in the western part of the country, is maintained by the United States federal government. These are public lands owned by all U.S. citizens. There are many kinds of federal lands. National parks, like Theodore Roosevelt National Park, are federal lands that are set aside so that they can be preserved. Other federal lands, such as national forests or national grasslands, are used in many different ways, including logging, ranching, and mining. Much of the land surrounding Theodore Roosevelt National Park is maintained by the government, including national grasslands and wildlife refuges.

Forest Service

The United States Department of Agriculture (USDA) Forest Service was started in 1905 to manage public lands in national forests and grasslands. The Forest Service today oversees an area of 191 million acres (77 million ha), which is an amount of land about the same size as Texas. In addition to protecting and managing America's public lands, the Forest Service also conducts forestry research and helps many state government and private forestry programs.

Glacier

A glacier is often called a river of ice. It is made of thick sheets of ice and snow. Glaciers slowly move downhill, scouring and smoothing the landscape.

Mesa

A mesa is a small, flat-topped hill with very steep sides. They are common in the American southwest, and in badland areas like those found in Theodore Roosevelt National Park.

Petrified Wood

Ancient wood that has had its cells replaced with mineral deposits. Stony chunks of petrified wood, millions of years old, are common in many areas of Theodore Roosevelt National Park.

Wetland

A wetland, sometimes called riparian, is an area of land that usually has standing water for most of the year, like swamps or marshes. Many wetlands have been set aside as preserves for wildlife. Many kinds of birds and animals depend on this habitat for nesting, food, and shelter.

Left: A summer sunset over the badlands of Theodore Roosevelt National Park.

Index